FOREVER BOUND

FOREVER BOUND

Poems from the Spouse of an Alzheimer's Sufferer

MICHAEL TARKA

PALMETTO
PUBLISHING
Charleston, SC
www.PalmettoPublishing.com

Copyright © 2024 by Michael Tarka

All rights reserved

No portion of this book may be reproduced, stored in a retrieval system, or transmitted in any form by any means—electronic, mechanical, photocopy, recording, or other—except for brief quotations in printed reviews, without prior permission of the author.

Paperback ISBN: 9798822965324

This book of poems is dedicated the bravest and strongest soul I know, my loving, beautiful wife Diane, to the multitude of spouses experiencing their own journeys with this evil disease, and finally to the the staff and caregivers at Olney Memory Care by ARTIS for taking care of Diane when I no longer could.

Diane I loved you yesterday, I love you today,
and I will love you forever.

*Your sons and daughters will prophesy,
your old men will dream dreams,
your young men will see visions.
Joel 3:1*

*The Lord God opened my ear:
I did not refuse,
Did not turn away.
Isaiah 50:5*

*I am my beloved's and my beloved is mine.
Song of Solomon 8:3*

*Love never fails.
1 Corinthians 13:8*

*For the greater the love the greater the grief,…
C. S. Lewis*

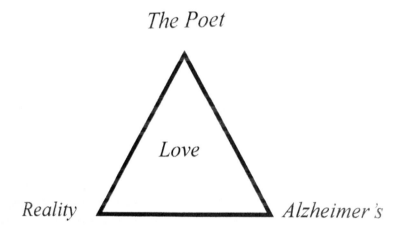

These poems touch on a triad of topics and concepts, all seemingly different yet all inter-related and in the center of the triad, love, which binds all three.

Acknowledgements

Special thank you's go to Lynette at Olney Memory Care by ARTIS, Sharon, my therapist who got me through the darkest crisis I have ever faced, and to Sterling, a long time air traffic controller friend who experienced a similar difficult journey with his wife, Karen, for reading these poems as I wrote them and assuring me I was not crazy. Your reactions and feedback helped me to understand that I needed to write these poems, and bring the collection to fruition in this book. I am definitely the reluctant poet, but sensed something beyond my understanding at work here while I wrote these poems.

To my son Geoff and my daughter Allison, I hope you find solace in this book knowing that the poems reflect my true deepest feelings for your mom. These poems also reflect how much this evil disease affected me as I tried to understand existential issues brought about by the changes caused by this disease, as well as being forced to recognize my failures and shortcomings in dealing with this disease. I love you both so much and so does your Mom.

Listen to the voice if it ever comes and visits you in your life. Writing this book has been a weird and amazing experience, something I was destined to do to draw attention to the millions suffering from this evil disease and those who give care to them whether families, friends, or professional staff. We all are humans, some of us are angels. These families and those who suffer need more angels.

Mike and Diane at her parent's house - 1979

Table of Contents

Introduction · 1
The Story Behind the Poems · 4
Essex Place · 10
I'll Never · 14
Forever Bound · 16
Moments · 19
The Picture · 22
Torn · 24
Abyss · 26
Rides · 28
Angels in Black · 30
A Voice from Behind the Veil · 32
Pathways · 34
Smile · 36
Feeding the Bride · 39
Relentlessly · 40
The Mist · 42
Stranger · 44
Last Lines · 46
Without You · 48
Solitude · 50
Millions of Voices · 52
The Poet · 54
I Pray · 56
About the Author: · 58

Introduction

Alzheimer's is the great thief. It steals the past, it steals the present, and it steals the future. It steals not only from the victim but from the spouse, children, siblings, and from society in general. It is a disease that steals hope and dreams, for there is no hope of preventing it, no hope of a cure, no hope of remission. It steals the health of not only the victims but the physical and mental health of their family caregivers.

Alzheimer's is an evil disease, a "cancer of the mind", knowing no boundaries of love, contributions to society, friendship, or past accomplishments. Like a tornado it creates devastation in its path; it creates hopelessness, despair, exhaustion, depression, and frustration in the victims and in their families and friends. Still glimmers of love, and golden moments peek through the darkness and must be cherished. Love survives forever.

I survived a major heart attack earlier this year because a "voice" commanded me to "Act now!", saving my life as I was starting to pass out. I responded to that command by calling 911. That "voice" was part of God's plan for me to continue to be here to support my wife, Diane. I believe God put our souls together for this moment in time. I believe our souls are intertwined, maybe a little bit of Diane's soul in me and a little bit of my soul in her. No question that she is more than just my physical wife, she is my soul mate.

I believe that I was destined to meet Diane just for the purpose of being here for her so that she would not have to go through this evil disease alone. There were six inflection points in my life that led the son of a Rhode Island steelworker to the daughter of a Tennessee postal worker. These six inflection points were tied to simple sentences spoken by different people:

- "Study hard, you are not going to do what I do for a living." (my father who spoke this was a steelworker, a dirty, hard, manual labor job). I focused on my studies.

- "Do you want to play golf with me?" (12 year old friend who turned me on to golf which kept me off the street corners). My teenage years were spent on the golf course where I met good people with values who cared for me and gave me summer jobs. Combined with my study habits I was able to get into Providence College, the first person in my family who went to college.

- "You are a psychology major." (Dr. Richard Lambe, Providence College). I could not say no to this professor as he had me sign a paper that changed my major from math to psychology.

- "You can study for the Graduate Record Exams." (Dr. George Raymond, Providence College). I did not know what the next step would be after studying psychology for four years, but becoming a professor like Rich and George intrigued me but first I had to take the GREs and score well enough to get into graduate school. So I studied hard for this standardized test and did well enough to get a fellowship to attend Vanderbilt University in Nashville, Tennessee.

- "Vanderbilt selected you first, why would you change your mind now?" (my mother). This is what my mother told me when I was considering a last minute offer from Indiana University. I chose Vanderbilt because of what she said, keeping me on track for Nashville.

- "Hey can you move in earlier to the duplex? There is a girl next door and I have been going over to talk with her a lot because I have no one here to talk to. I already have a girlfriend and should not be going over as much as I have been." (Ray D., my graduate school roommate and fellow Providence College graduate). I agreed to move up my move in date. The girl Ray referred to was Diane.

As you can see the above were subtle, simple sentences that changed the course of my life to stay on God's plan for me. These inflection points kept me on a path from an early age that led a steelworker's son from Rhode Island to meet a postal worker's daughter from Nashville, get married, raise a family, and be together to endure this evil disease.

The Story Behind the Poems

The first poem, "Essex Place", describes the time from initially meeting Diane to marrying her. The next three poems, "I'll Never", "Forever Bound", and "Moments" deal with loss, and my struggles to reconcile the finality I am facing with the continued love that I have for Diane. I asked God three questions:

- Will Diane continue to love me after she passes from this life?

- Is our marriage over when she passes, is this it, the best is behind us?

- Why did I survive my heart attack, what's my purpose going forward?

I did not realize until after I had completed these three poems that the last line of each contained my answers:

- I'll love you forever, because love never ends.

- A marriage of souls, forever bound.

- Light a candle in someone's life, fill the darkness on the Candle Path.

"The Picture" is a poem about one of those candle moments. A picture arrived from out of the blue from a bridesmaid compelled to send it to me. The picture captures a moment in time with so many intense feelings: love, happiness, and hope. This poem represents a poetic translation of that picture.

"Torn" was the most difficult poem to write as it expresses my deepest feelings when Diane was initially diagnosed (the day I was "torn") and during my subsequent caregiving efforts. "Abyss" describes the constant struggle of living life at the edge of an emotional abyss.

The poem "Rides", expresses how our experience of reality is influenced by others. The same road traveled but not the same reality experienced.

"Angels in Black" is a poem about surrendering Diane's care to a memory care facility. It focuses on accepting that caregiving is best done by angels. The next several poems, "A Voice from Behind the Veil", "Pathways", and "Feeding the Bride" are reflections on the time I spend with Diane each day at lunch at the memory care facility. "Pathways" and "Feeding the Bride" point out that there are deeper ways to view the reality we sometimes only see in a mundane way, such as pushing a wheelchair or feeding a loved one. "Smile" also has given me a deeper appreciation for the significance of a simple act, smiling.

	Surface Processing of Reality	**Deep Processing of Reality**
Reality Experienced Alone	Reality not colored by others, the mundane reality we exist in most of the time where we transit through reality to accomplish some goal, simple existence.	Reality personally experienced at a much deeper level of understanding, and insight, not colored by the presence of another. Reality where deepest emotions reside and where sensitivity to the meaning of our surroundings and activities can be accessed.
Reality Experienced With Others	Reality may not be colored by presence of others in our life or only minimally. Like above, the reality when we are "going through the motions" except in this case we are sharing our experience with others who may or may not minimally influence our perception/experience of reality.	All of the above plus Reality is colored by others and experienced at the deepest level because of their presence. "I see things differently when I am with you." This is the Full Reality that can be experienced with a true soulmate.

THE FOUR WAYS OF EXPERIENCING REALITY

"Relentlessly" was scribbled in the sand with a stick as I watched the ocean waves pound the beach on a bad surf day. In this poem, I saw similarities between what the ocean was doing to the beach and what Alzheimer's relentless attacks were doing to Diane's mind/brain."The Mist" came to me as I was taking a long early morning walk on the beach. I was watching couple after couple walk past me going in the opposite direction. Meanwhile, in front of me up the beach a misty haze clouded the beach. I was thinking of Diane and how we had walked this beach and how much I missed her and loved her. I just happened to look down at that point and noticed a large shell fragment in the shape of a heart. I took it as a sign. This poem tumbled out of that experience.

Sometimes Alzheimer's sufferers do not recognize their spouses as the disease progresses. "Stranger" addresses that situation. The Poet came to me on two consecutive nights while I was sleeping, persistent in its direction for me to write a poem titled "Stranger", the first five lines coming to me as I slept. I finally acquiesced.

The poem titled "Last Lines" is a poem focusing on the last line of eleven of the poems. The last line of each poem provided an answer, a direction, or a question yet not answered and that may not be answered in this life.

"Without You" is a projection into my future when I will truly be without Diane, the Disease taking its victory lap. It is unclear why "Stranger" and "Without You" needed to be written at this time, as they both delve into future scenarios. Again I felt compelled to write them now.

"Solitude" is motivated by a dream where I clearly saw the words "ALL ALONE" emblazoned on a golf bag. This is the only poem where I chose the title as opposed to being provided a title by the Poet as is true for each of the other poems.

"Millions of Voices" reflects that even though we can feel like we are taking this Alzheimer's journey alone, there are millions of spouses, family and friends of Alzheimer's sufferers experiencing the same deep emotions as we are experiencing. For me, these poems are the result of a "poetic lens" focusing the feelings of millions.

The next to last poem, "The Poet", is a recognition that I am a reluctant poet with no love of poetry or skill in writing poetry. The Poet mined my soul, exposing regrets and extracting feelings, that I either was unaware of or did not want to admit existed.

Prior to this book, I have not written a poem in over 55 years. Every poem in this book was inspired, and communicated to me through dreams, images and just lines of poetry popping into my head, like some poetic data dump. I really can only take credit for taking dictation and not for any creativity reflected in these poems. I know this sounds weird and it is weird to me but it is truthful.

I have also noticed that my relationship to the Poet has evolved. Initially it was more direct, in your face, type of communication as if the door to the Poet was rusty and needed extra force to be opened. The instructions to write the first poem, "I'll Never" came in a vivid instructional dream unlike any other dream that I have experienced. The Poet showed me a piece of paper (yellow lined) with the title "I'll Never" written in cursive in blue ink at the top of the piece of paper. The Poet repeatedly asked me "Do you understand, the title will be "I'll Never?" and then "Do you have it, "I'll Never?". Only after I confirmed that I understood did the next set of instructions come telling me that each line of the poem should begin with or contain the words "I'll never", followed by three lines of the poem to make sure I understood what my task was to be. I joked with a friend that "God writes in cursive".

Subsequent poems, title and all, came verbally into my brain while awake usually at the most inopportune times, like when I was driving, putting away groceries, or pushing Diane's wheel chair around the gardens at the memory care facility. One poem came as a vivid image while I was sitting in my backyard looking at the trees. Still another poem came from a picture that one of Diane's bridesmaids was "compelled" to send me when I thought I was done writing poems.

Now, the Poet's communications are more subtle and softer, waiting for me to ask for help, to say that I am ready to receive. The voice now less forceful and more soft, a helper vs a director. Imagine a form of communication so powerful that it led me to write a book of poems exposing my truest and deepest emotions regards Diane's and my Alzheimers journey. It does make me wonder who The Poet really is that they could compel me to write the first poem, all subsequent ones, and then this book. The direct to mind form of communication of the Poet was eerily similar to the communication to "act now" when I was suffering my heart attack. It makes me wonder if the communicator in these two separate set of events was the same or at least a similar being.

Finally, the last poem, "I Pray", are my prayers for you, me and all the sufferers of this evil disease. This is not only the last poem of the book but one of the last poems that I wrote. I believe that the Poet was telling me he is not the end here, and that prayer is all we have in the end to get through this journey.

Essex Place

Author's note: This poem was a reward to me after writing the poem "Torn". I had asked the Poet to give me a break as the deep dive I had taken into the emotional, dark times recounted in "Torn" were still wearing on me. The Poet responded with "Essex Place", the only poem in the collection that covers a time not impacted by Alzheimer's. It represents what happened when I first met Diane to our marriage, the happiest time in my life. Such simple happiness, not a happiness of wealth, power, and things, but a happiness of holding hands, kissing, walks, cooking, friends, and each other. Happiness from little money.

The Journey started on Essex Place, one sultry, Nashville summer afternoon,
The first time we met a long embrace, I remember how you felt pressed against me,
Feelings came across me that I had never met anyone like you before; you were different,
Your smile, your face, I felt something special, I just wanted to be with you,
You made me comfortable, putting my shyness at ease.

You asked me out on our first date, although we never really dated in the traditional sense,
You were literally the girl next door,
We always just hung out together, deciding what we were going to do next,

FOREVER BOUND

I still remember my nerves before that first date, my first time to be
 truly alone with you,
As we always had a crowd on my side of the house on Essex,
Thinking, "Don't mess this up!"
A work picnic for you in the country side,
Spent most of our time together holding hands, talking and sneaking in
 kisses,
Neither trying to impress the other, using the picnic as a vehicle to
 spend time together.

A short time later you left on a trip you had planned before we met,
Later you told me that you were thinking of cancelling,
When you left, I experienced feelings that I did not recognize,
I missed you dearly, I could not stop thinking of you,
Feelings like something had been stolen from me for that week,
It was Love, real Love, not puppy love, infatuation or any other cheap
 imitation,
Zero to Love in a couple of months.

Love was confirmed with the joy I experienced on your return,
Hearing from you that you also experienced the same feelings and
 thoughts,
No more trips apart from each other,
We were bound by Love.

The portal between the two sides of the house on Essex Place saw a lot
 of traffic,
At times I was confused which side I actually lived on,
But simplified the complexities that can come with dating,
No need to call, texting wasn't an option,
I just walked through the portal, we could not bear being separated.

Walks to Centennial Park, tossing a Frisbee,
Spending our last five dollars on a red one that I still have,

Miniature golf nights, carving pumpkins,
Camping in Cades Cove, riding bicycles in the rain,
Spending a Sunday afternoon at a garage behind a pig farm getting your car repaired,
Walks around Essex Place, holding hands, petting Marigold, talking to neighbors,
Goo Goo clusters, the Pancake House,
Simple pleasures, no need to impress.

Occasionally we would dress up to go out, a restaurant, a concert, Grand Ole Opry,
I was so blessed, so lucky to have you walk by my side,
You were truly beautiful.

Never formally asked you to marry me,
We just started making plans, less than six months after our initial embrace,
Less than one year later, "I do",
Another sultry, Nashville summer afternoon,
Full of friends and family and a car covered in whipped cream, and candy as we left the reception in the summer heat,
Thousands of ants taking up residence as the car sat during our honeymoon.

Is yesterday gone forever?
I long to return to those magical, simpler times when love was ignited and flourished on Essex Place.

FOREVER BOUND

Diane during our days at Essex Place - 1980

I'll Never

Author's Note: A poem about what I had, what I lost, and what I keep forever in the end. The idea for and writing of this poem was inspired by a communication in a dream instructing me to write a poem titled "I'll Never", providing me instructions that each line must contain "I'll Never". The communication gave me several example lines to clarify what I was to do. That dream/communication woke me up from a sound sleep one morning at 5:00 AM. I hope I did justice to the communication in the dream as I am not a poet and do not even like poetry but I was compelled to do this. I do not know why.

I'll never forget the first time we met, a magical embrace,
I'll never forget the smile on your face.

I'll never forget the sound of your voice,
I'll never forget the joy that you brought me.

I'll never forget the kisses we shared,
I'll never forget falling in love with you.

I'll never forget looking into your eyes thinking how lucky I am,
I'll never forget the time we spent together, the joy it brought me just to
    be with you.

I'll never forget what I am no longer able to do with you,
I'll never forget what we have lost.

FOREVER BOUND

I'll never again enjoy the beach with you,
I'll never again have you reach for my hand.

I'll never snuggle with you on the couch again,
I'll never hold you in my arms again.

I'll never dine with you again,
I'll never share a glass of wine with you again.

I'll never again go for a walk with you, holding hands,
I'll never again have a good talk with you.

I'll never again start or end my day with you,
I'll never feel the same again.

I'll love you forever, because love never ends.

Forever Bound

Author's Note—A poem whose first 3 lines were deposited in my mind suddenly while I was driving to the grocery store. Upon arriving at home I typed the first 3 lines that I had been given and proceeded to put away groceries, occasionally interrupted by the receipt of more lines. Over the course of 2-3 hours this poem was written in several 2-3 minute spurts, tears welling up as I typed these lines. It was like I was taking dictation and the poem was writing itself.

Our souls are intertwined,
Part of my soul lives in you,
Part of your soul lives in me,
Yesterday, today, tomorrow,
Entangled forever.

Before we met, our souls had a hole,
Waiting to be filled,
I remember the instant yours filled mine,
Beyond love, it was completion of me,
I can only pray that I completed you.

As I write, tears fill me, telling me all said above is true,
My soul longs to be with you,
Beyond the corporeal, loves run deep,
For it is at that level that souls truly meet,
Once entangled no man can tear asunder.

FOREVER BOUND

Even though this Evil strangles your mind,
I know deep inside you that your soul still shines,
And somewhere in there is the entanglement of our souls,
Created by God and sustained by our love,
For this Evil cannot strangle your soul.

"For richer, for poorer",
"In sickness and in health",
Those are words for this world,
Death cannot split us apart,
A marriage of souls, forever bound.

MICHAEL TARKA

Diane at Olney Memory Care by ARTIS
July 2024 on her 72nd birthday

Moments

Author's Note- This poem came in the form of an image while I was sitting quietly in the backyard.

Candles stretching forward and behind in a long path in the darkness,
Nothing but candles flickering and darkness,
Each candle a moment in time cherished,
Darkness fills the voids between the candles,
The darkness of hurt and the routines and sometimes mindlessness of our daily existence.

I walk the Candle Path, behind me memories of moments past,
Ahead of me moments yet to be experienced,
There are times when the next candle is but a short journey,
Other times the darkness envelops me,
The candles behind and in front of me just a minuscule glow.

I long for the next moment, the soft glow of another candle,
A hug, a hand squeeze, a gaze, a kind action or words given or received,
All we have in life is moments,
With age and illness the candles seem to get fewer and further between,
Blessed by candles in the past and hope for candles in the future.

Life is a journey through this cosmic row of candles and darkness,
Tomorrow's candles are already out there waiting to be discovered,
Yesterday's candles are not gone forever waiting to be remembered,

I search for the next candle, the next golden moment when I visit you,
For I not know when it will come, as the voids can be great.

The darkness is an opportunity for the existence of another candle,
Candles exist in pairs, one on the path of the moment giver, one on the
    path of the moment recipient,
You filled my life with candles, the Path illuminated by special
    moments,
You saved me from darkness, a lonely, meaningless journey through life,
Know that when all else fails.

Light a candle in someone's life, fill the darkness on the Candle Path.

THE PICTURE - MIKE AND DIANE - JULY 1980 -
THE LOOK OF TRUE LOVE AND HAPPINESS.

The Picture

A bridesmaid compelled to find pictures of us now, why,
I opened the envelope and there it is,
One look and a rogue wave of emotions overpowers me,
I cannot contain the tears, a simple moment frozen in time.

How deep is the well in my soul?
The picture drawing from depths unimaginable,
A purging of feelings residing in the core.

Your hand around me, resting on my shoulder,
Looking into each other's eyes, each other's souls,
Nothing else in the world mattered in that instant when the shutter clicked,
Your smile sparkling, eyes like diamonds, love vibrating in the gap between us, around us,
Hope blanketing us, pure happiness in that moment.

I desperately want to recreate that image, that moment,
I want to feel what I felt in that picture,
I want to see what I saw in that picture,
I want your arm around me, hand on my shoulder,
I want to live that moment again.

Tomorrow has already occurred and yesterday is not gone forever,
A twelve year old boy wrote those words over fifty years ago,
Would you come back with me if we could, or am I just delusional,

FOREVER BOUND

But I cannot even ask you now as the Disease has stolen wishful thinking among its many spoils.

How did we get here so soon,
Where yesterday is brighter than tomorrow,
I am feeling pulled toward the light of yesterday,
Being pulled into this candle,
Did not understand candles have depth,
The feelings embedded in the picture deep within the candle.

Torn

The ripping sound that day I was torn,
Tried to stay strong for you, a facade of strength on the outside, failing miserably on the inside,
Initial surge of adrenaline to solve this problem, a marathon faced me, but I started sprinting,
Made promises to myself that I could not keep,
Quickly devolved into a nosedive through darkness that I could not even imagine existed.

No one to help, hope deserted me,
Could not wait for you to call it a day so I could call it a day and catch a break,
Hated mornings because it brought unknowns,
Evolved to caregiver more than husband, always longing to be just a husband again,
In sickness and in health, but we were pronounced husband and wife, not caregiver and wife.

It was like the Disease knew when I was at my weakest, most tired, to manifest the next decline or incident,
Thought there was an "S" on my chest,
But manifested only an explosion inside my chest.

At wit's end, I could not deal with this any more, I wanted to run away like a little boy,
Maybe I was running back to be a little boy again,

FOREVER BOUND

Safe from the harsh realities of failing you; I am so sorry,
Said things that I did not mean, acted in ways that I regret; I am so sorry,
Forgive me.

This evil Disease changed me in ways that I could not even imagine,
Just as you could never imagine going through something like this,
I wish I were more of an angel than a human in those tough times.

Echoes from that day continue now like aftershocks,
Softer over time but always present,
The tear still there, open for me only to see,
The darkness on the periphery, at bay, but always ready to consume again.

The Disease wins, but it is not a gracious winner, it pokes a finger in your eyes and laughs at your efforts to beat it,
It continues to remind you everyday, you lost, I won,
What will mend me?
Or am I forever torn.

Abyss

Dancing on the rim of an abyss,
Winds of emotion have me teetering on the edge,
Only head winds pushing towards the abyss,
The abyss, a place where you don't care about yourself anymore,
Once ended up there when my spouse could not take care of herself anymore,
When I could not take care of her anymore.

I don't know who I am at times,
I wander around aimlessly, trying to comprehend why,
What cosmic purpose is served by her suffering,
Is this suffering our penance?
I wonder as I dance on the rim of an abyss.

Put in a position where I could not save a love one,
A position where I am struggling to save myself,
Just wanted You to touch her and heal her,
I teeter on the edge,
Cries for help deep inside, cries for help break the silence,
I need you God, where are you?
I ponder the question as I dance on the rim of an abyss.

So confused at times, the darkness of the abyss always in the periphery now,
Looking not to misstep again, the abyss forever ready to swallow me again,

FOREVER BOUND

My mind struggling, my soul struggling,
I cannot flounder as I dance on the rim of an abyss.

Slowly I try to step back but geysers of guilt and sadness erupt blocking
    my way,
Forcing me back to the rim of an abyss,
Searching for the pathway, sometimes I feel trapped at the rim,
Head winds preventing me from turning away,
I am tired, no longer do I want to dance at the rim of an abyss.

Rides

Sixties music on the radio, vistas of trees and farmland outside the windows,
I am trying to escape and am taking you with me,
But this Disease is like a hitchhiker in the back seat of the car,
As we ride to nowhere in particular, I wonder if we can drop him off at the next turn,
He lurks back there, eyes peering at us and a constant hand on your shoulder.

I am searching for a reprieve, a golden moment when we are not burdened by the hitchhiker in the back seat,
Where we can enjoy what remains of our precious time together, so short,
A few moments of normal is all I seek,
Something I can grasp on to as you slip away from me.

Curvy back roads, no traffic,
I drive slowly so you can admire the scenery,
On the horizon, a farm with horses,
I slow down and lower the window for you to say sweet nothings to them.
I see the joy in your eyes and the smile on your face,
The hitchhiker asleep in the back for several moments.

A field of golden sunflowers smiling at us in the summer sun,
Crimson leaves on a lone tree contrasting with the fall sky,

FOREVER BOUND

A snow covered landscape, no one else on the road,
The beauty of silence, the landscape covered in pure white,
The peacefulness in your eyes as the miles pass, as the seasons pass.

I no longer can drive those same roads without looking over at your empty seat,
Remembering what was, imagining what could have been,
Sometimes it is more than I can bear,
Emotions of "this is not the same", "this is not right" flood me, as the tires hum,
The same beautiful scenery that I traveled with you now a monochrome of grays and impure whites.

You no longer beside me to color my reality.

Angels in Black

I am searching for angels, praying for angels to be with you,
I am sorry that I cannot always be there with you, be there for you,
I tried to be your angel, but I always seemed to come up short,
Limits reached, goals not reached.

If not me how can I trust someone else,
For alone I am destined to fail you and me,
I surrender,
Difficult to surrender control, but underestimated the care you would need,
I search for the perfect place for you, not knowing perfection is unattainable,
Rather should be searching for love and caring, for those are the goals now.

Overwhelmed by the decision I needed to make,
Not just a decision of feeding, bathing, and dressing, but a decision of caring, loving, and respect,
I am hoping for angels to come into your life,
Angels do not always have wings, angels do not always wear white,
Sometimes the angels we need to take care of our loved ones are dressed in black,
Angels in black now doing what I no longer can do.

"I just want to go home", softly said,
You are home, a new home,

FOREVER BOUND

My heart breaks.

Angels are not needed for the easy things, angels do hard things,
Caregiving is hard, caregiving a spouse is heart breaking,
Surrendering caregiving not an admission of failure, its an admission of human limitations,
I try to convince myself of that, sometimes I am successful.

A Voice from Behind the Veil

"My hubby is here! Everyone, my hubby is here!"
The joy in your eyes, the smile on your face,
Laughter in the dining room, as your voice exclaims my arrival,
A candle in my darkness, the Veil penetrated by your words and your smile,
"I love it when you are with me".

A tender touch, a kiss, as we wait for lunch to arrive,
And once again,
"I just love being with you"
A sense of relief spreads over you, for you are no longer alone with the Veil,
Brought about by the simple act of me being there to share a moment in time.

Although the Veil fosters isolation and loneliness, the Veil still lifts for Love,
"You don't know how much I love you"
As carrots, and bits of turkey and berries go from the fork I hold to your mouth,
"My babe!"
"You're the best-est"
Dessert comes, my presence a small sacrifice, rewarded by the lifting of the Veil.

FOREVER BOUND

"Never in my whole life did I ever imagine going through something like this",
My jaw drops, your true voice returning,
A sad realization when I was hoping your awareness had been muted,
Living in the moment, rather than introspecting on a situation that cannot be imagined, only experienced,
The Veil lifted, a slip in its armor,
Your true self, sparkling for an instant, only to once again be covered by the Veil.

How long will you be able to penetrate the Veil, lifting it briefly to show the light that is you,
If I could I would hold the Veil open for you, but strength is not what lifts the Veil,
Determination, grit and fortitude are not what lifts the Veil,
I want to remove that damn Veil so much,
Love is the only thing under your control that still lifts the Veil,
"I love you so so much, I don't know what I'd do without you"

Pathways

Author's Note: Pathways is a poem about my daily activity of pushing Diane's wheel chair around the fenced in backyard of the facility and in the inside hallways. There is a door that separates the lobby from the resident's area. That is the mundane world explanation of what I do. The poem describes a different level of meaning that I was made aware of in writing this poem. Writing this poem made me aware that reality can be explained in a set of mundane actions or at a deeper level that has more significant meaning.

Pathways to nowhere, sun beaming down us,
We traverse the pathways that have been defined for us,
Taking in the scenery along the path, but dare not stray,
Plants with leaves like elephant ears, flowers the size of your hand,
A carpet of dandelions, fall leaves color the sky, you wave at the flowers.

Seasons pass but the pathways do not change,
The scenery provides a degree of normalcy, perhaps even temporary
    happiness,
Masking the cold, stark finiteness of the Pathway for those who walk it.

Beautiful barriers isolate and protect those on the pathways, shrinking
    and constraining reality,
A reminder of the constraints on the minds of those who travel the
    pathways,
Flowers, trees, birds, bees, colors, warmth, a cool breeze out here,
Contrasts with the relative starkness of the Pathway to nowhere in there.

FOREVER BOUND

We encounter other faces on the pathways,
Walking on their own journey, with their own thoughts and feelings,
Some days there are many on the pathways, other days we travel in solitude,
Wondering if this is all there is, a future defined by the pathways,
For hope is not an exit on these pathways.

In time we transition pathways, the sun and flowers transitioning to the walls and floors that protect those on this parallel pathway to nowhere,
Round and round we go,
Stopping to admire the changing scenery through the glass portals,
Longing to be anywhere but nowhere.

The time comes, I must leave you,
We exit the pathway at a stop where your day will continue,
I kiss you goodbye and return to the pathway.

I press the button, another pathway reveals itself,
Not a pathway to nowhere but a pathway to everywhere,
I step through the opening onto the pathway knowing that you no longer can follow me.

Smile

I walk into the room and sit down next to you,
The curvature of your lips,
The sparkle in your eyes,
A smile that reminds me of the first day we met,
A smile conveying so much to me, happiness in the moment, love,
A simple smile from you is what I live for,
A smile surviving the onslaught of this evil Disease.

Not happiness from wealth, power, accumulation of things, just happiness from a simple smile,
A smile from you brings about lightness in the air, a lightness in my step,
A smile adding brightness to an already sunny day,
A smile to nourish me, so that I do not fell empty when I leave you.

The emotions of watching a loved one suffer drowning me at times,
A smile is a life preserver that keeps me afloat,
Your smile and words lighting up the dining room,
Creating a wave of smiles from others,
Smiles are contagious.

I look at your engagement photo, a smile on your face,
Your face has changed but the smile has not,
Smiles are not affected by time,
The same smile before our wedding day as I see now in the dining room,

FOREVER BOUND

So much emotion conveyed in that simple smile.

I fell in love with that smile,
I am still in love with that smile,
That smile like an anesthetic, numbing all the negative emotions,
I smile.

Help your loved one smile, it may make you smile too.

Diane's captivating smile then in her engagement photo and now - August 2024

MICHAEL TARKA

DIANE AND MIKE ON THEIR WEDDING DAY- 1980

Feeding the Bride

Fed you cake on our wedding day,
Fed you lunch on the day of our forty fourth anniversary,
A promise fulfilled,
Pictures of our wedding on your lap, as I fed you dessert,
Groom once again, feeding his bride.

Each day at lunch, a celebration of our wedding day, through such a simple act,
An expression of my love for you,
The reason why I am still here,
The reason why I was destined to be here.

No longer can I dress, you, bathe you, meet your daily needs,
Your physical needs exceeding my physical capabilities,
Except for this simple act of compassion and love,
In sickness and in health I can still feed you, the lifting of a fork to your mouth not beyond my physical limitations.

That wedding picture in your lap, changed my reality,
Once was a task, now a celebration of our wedding each day that I feed you,
I did not understand,
I do now.

Relentlessly

Relentlessly the waves of the ocean pounding the beaches of your mind,
Water rising and crashing down, white caps depositing tangles of seaweed on the shore,
Each set followed by another,
In a never ending barrage of the beach.

Water receding, sand being pulled grain by grain, cell by cell, from the beaches,
Slowly but relentlessly the ocean erodes the beaches of your mind,
Leaving behind only those tangles of seaweed, and piles of driftwood covered in the plaque of the sea.

Calming at times, the waves smaller with greater spacing,
A break in the barrage,
The flotsam and jetsam not being churned from the bottom,
Your life stabilizes, but the beach is not cleaned of all that has been deposited.

The winds pick up, the sea starts churning,
Waves swelling, water crashing,
More tangles of seaweed wash up on the beach,
More sand washes away.

The beach becomes smaller,
Grains of sand surrendered to the ocean,
Forever lost,

FOREVER BOUND

Each grain a cell in your mind.

All sea,
No beach,
Just tangles of seaweed as the ocean recedes.

The Mist

Early morning,
Couples walking on the beach towards me,
The way God intended, they are one,
I, however, am walking in the opposite direction,
Alone in my thoughts, in my prayers.

I do not know what to pray for, as I see another couple approaching,
I think of you, of us,
Still a couple and yet not,
I walk alone.

In front of me in the distance the mist blurs the details of the beach,
I alone walk towards the mist,
A future unclear, shrouded in unknowns,
The string of couples behind me now,
In front of me only an empty beach, and the mist.

The waves rolling ashore,
Shell fragments crunching under my feet,
I look down,
At my feet is a heart shape fragment of shell,
Mere coincidence that I arrived at that spot to look down?
Or is the shell a communication of something deeper?
From whom?
Perhaps you sent me to that spot.

FOREVER BOUND

I pick up the shell, its shape a symbol of love,
Our love,
A reminder of us, a reminder of our love, before I enter the mist.

Stranger

Author's Note: Sometimes Alzheimer's sufferers do not recognize their spouses as the disease progresses. This poem addresses that situation. The Poet came to me on two consecutive nights while I was sleeping, persistent in its direction for me to write a poem titled Strangers, the first 5 lines coming to me as I slept. I finally acquiesced.

Stranger,
Friend,
Lover,
Husband,
Stranger.

The cycle is complete, the universe reset,
The Disease steals the precious thing that we held on to,
The last bond between us
The essence of Us stolen by It.

I a stranger to you,
You a soulmate to me,
The Disease does not understand that you and I both contain a
    repository of the Us,
No joint Us now, just the Us retained by me.

It cannot steal my memories of Us,
It cannot steal our entangled souls,

FOREVER BOUND

It cannot steal the imprint our love made on our friends, our family,
    this world, this universe.

The Disease's last attempt to have me abandon you,
To let go,
For my ties to you are stronger than your ties to me right now,
I recognize It does not have control over me, if I do not cede control,
I know the truth, I am not a stranger,
I am your friend, lover, and husband, Us exists in me.

I will not let go.

Last Lines

I long to return to those magical, simpler times when love was ignited and flourished on Essex Place,
Love so pure, love so simple, love so deep,
If only we could return to those days,
Is yesterday gone forever, am I fool longing to go back?

I step through the opening onto the pathway knowing that you no longer can follow me,
You no longer beside me to color my reality,
Our paths diverging, my reality shifting,
Not ready for this,
Life is just not the same without you, my reality dimmer, less vibrant.

I'll love you forever, because love never ends,
A marriage of souls, forever bound,
"I love you so so much, I don't know what I'd do without you",
Answers to questions asked as I talk into the void of an empty house,
True love is not bound by the temporal nature of our existence,
Love transcends time, love creates a permanent bond,
I don't know where I would be without you,
I don't know what I would do without you, I am scared to find out,
I hope the comfort of our love sustains me.

I try to convince myself of that, sometimes I am successful,
Or am I forever torn,
Doubts fill my mind, a rollercoaster of emotions,

FOREVER BOUND

I did my best, I did not,
I made the right decision, I did not.

Light a candle in someone's life, fill the darkness on the Candle Path,
I am still here because I have candles to light,
Candles for you, perhaps candles for others,
As you lit candles in my life.

And hopefully continues to be there as the Journey continues,
The Poet and these poems dove deep into me, pulling out what was
    deeply buried,
Hidden to even me,
For what purpose I do not know, maybe some day clarity will come,
Until then the Journey continues, insights and comfort gifted through
    simple poems.

Without You

I am scared, scared of life without you,
Writing this poem while you are still with me,
Not sure why I am writing a poem about being without you,
Again was given the title, awaiting the lines,
Don't know where this is going.

In some sense I am without you now,
"I want to go home", but I have to leave without you,
Tears me apart, angry at God for being without you.

I hurt so much, my soul is wounded,
Hurt is a by product of love when bad things happen,
The hurt is proportional to the love.

I am so alone, empty on the inside and on the outside,
Will I be able to go on?
Forty five years with you, I cannot comprehend "without you",

I go to embrace you but you are not there,
Can you hear me?
Can you see me?
Cannot fathom an end to our story,
Watch over me,
As I no longer can watch over you,
I cry, not a few tears but the crying equivalent of a belly laugh.

FOREVER BOUND

I write this poem not in the shoes of those who have lost spouses to this
    Evil,
Knowing some day I will be,
The Poet communicating what the future brings for me,
What the past was for many readers of His words.

Know that the words of these poems are for you and not just for me,
Know that He is with you as He has been with me.

Solitude

A dream haunts me, a golf bag stitched with the words "ALL ALONE",
Is this a foreshadowing of my future?
Maybe that is my destiny on the golf course, maybe that is my destiny in life,

I open the door, a symphony of silence playing loudly,
The house feels empty like it has lost its soul, I feel like a caretaker,
In the past a vivacious home, now just a dwelling,
Memories embedded in the walls.

Sometimes I go outside hoping to see a neighbor, just not to be all alone,
Conversation, human interaction, never thought as an only child I would crave it so much,
Solitude not peaceful but nerve wracking,
Find myself pacing like a caged animal, unable to be comfortable with my solitude, with myself.

I talk with God, He is a good listener but not much of a conversationalist,
My words bouncing off the walls back to me,
Echoes of solitude,
The phone does not ring, the doorbell never pressed,
Family and friends at a distance, I really wish they were all nearby.

FOREVER BOUND

Always had visions, dreams of you and I walking into the sunset hand in hand,
I wanted a happy ending, did not choose solitude, did not wish this Evil ending on a loved one,
This Evil Disease is like a horror movie unfolding, never knowing when the monster will pop up out of the shadows,
I wish that I could wish this all away.

I struggle without you, a life where I fear that I will be all alone.

Millions of Voices

I hurt,
I cannot be the only one who feels like this,
Millions of voices crying out "I hurt",
Feel like a lens, channeling the emotions of these millions into simple poetry,
If my hurt is so deep, so overwhelming at times, it is no wonder that the universe cries out with the hurt of the millions.

Connected with an entity not of flesh and blood,
Communications not of this world, but part of my world,
Dreams and images, instructions communicated, conversations had,
Clearly, concisely articulated, instantly in my mind,
Direct to the mind poetic data dumps,
Emotions of millions of voices manifested one line of poetry at a time.

Communications so compelling, so efficient,
Unbounded by time and events here on earth,
Coming while sleeping, driving, walking and sitting,
Could not ignore, could not say "No",
Determined to have me execute this task,
Relentless task master once the door was opened.

Going deeper and deeper into my soul,
Forcing me to purge feelings, I feel sick to my stomach at times,
I feel lost, yet the poems continue to arrive,

FOREVER BOUND

Bearing my soul, ripping my soul,
Cleansing me for some reason yet to be known.

The cry of millions echoing through the words I write,
The cry of one echoing through the words I write,
I hurt.

The Poet

Author's Note: All of these poems just came to me, I was given the titles and most if not all of the lines just came to me. For example, "Pathways "came to me as I was pushing Diane's wheelchair, I was writing things down on my hand, pieces of cloth, and scraps of paper. The first line and the last three lines of "Pathways" were written in a couple of instants, less than a minute. It was just like some poetic data dump from an external source. This is a poem about my experiences as a reluctant poet.

I am but an instrument of the Poet,
A holder of the pen, a mind to receive and transcribe poetic lines,
Poems coming in dreams with titles written in cursive,
Poems coming in images with titles arriving in my mind almost
    magically,
Lines arriving in groups between mundane daily chores,
I am compelled to respond, I cannot ignore.

Why was I, who does not read or write poetry, chosen to be an
    instrument of the Poet,
To take his dictation, transcribing thoughts arriving faster than I can
    capture at times,
My mind racing to repeat the phrases or my hands being used both as
    scribe and as the paper for recording when nothing else is available,
For the Poet communicates at a different level and speed than you and
    I,
The transfer of thoughts, concepts, lines directly to the mind,

FOREVER BOUND

I find I cannot keep up at times as poetry essence fills my mind.

Every poem title supplied by the Poet,
Every line dictated by, motivated by or gist provided by the Poet,
The Poet reads my mind as each poem answers a question or provides direction,
This is poetry on a cosmic plane for what purpose I still do not know.

I still long for the days of life without poetry,
Days of hugs, kisses, smiles, a hand held, simple pleasures, comforting pleasures,
But maybe I was destined to encounter the Poet,
For he comes not to those who do not have a need for him,
I am thankful that in my time of need the Poet was there,
And hopefully continues to be there as the Journey continues.

I Pray

I pray for the millions of voices crying out,
I hope you find comfort for your hurt.

I pray for the sufferers of this evil disease,
I hope you know that you are loved deeply.

I pray for the lives, marriages, and relationships stolen,
I hope you know that love survives.

I pray that you find moments of happiness,
I hope someone lights a candle in your life.

I pray for the professional caregivers to whom we have entrusted our loved ones,
I hope you now understand why we need angels, may you be blessed with the strength, compassion and love of an angel.

I pray for those who walk on the rim of the abyss,
I hope you never fall into the deep despair and darkness.

I pray for you who are all alone,
I hope that the light of family and friends shine through the solitude.

I pray that my truthfulness and honesty about my feelings allow you to examine your feelings,
I hope your examination allows you to go forward unshackled.

FOREVER BOUND

I pray that any emotional scars from taking care of a loved one heal,
I hope that you know that you did your best, best is not perfect, best is
    not some ideal in a movie.

I pray for a miracle,
I hope that I can see a world where this "cancer of the mind" is
    eradicated.

I pray that these poems have made a difference to those on this journey,
I hope that you pray for me, for in the end all we have left is prayer.

About the Author:

Dr. Michael Tarka is a retired human factors engineer. His distinguished 40-year career was spent developing, maintaining, and enhancing our nation's air traffic control system.

Six years ago, he was thrust into the role of caregiver as his wife, Diane, of 38 years was diagnosed with Alzheimer's disease. Together, they have two grown children.

Milton Keynes UK
Ingram Content Group UK Ltd.
UKHW021645011224
451755UK00011B/816